The Headless Oxman Study Guide

General Education Edition

5th Grade Level

P.K Burian & K.P. Azeltine

Student Packet

Written by

P.K Burian & M.E. Drewry

NOTE TO THE TEACHER

This reproducible study guide consists of lessons to use in conjunction with the specific novel, The Headless Oxman. Written in a chapter-by-chapter format, the study guide contains reading, vocabulary, writing, comprehension, literary, science and fun words exercises to use as a follow-up to the novel.

This study guide can be used in a class instruction or in reading groups at their appropriate reading levels. Depending on the amount of time devoted to reading in the classroom, each book with its study guide and lessons can be completed in three to six weeks.

Begin by tying the novel for reading development by passing out the book and a folder to each student. Hand out duplicated pages of the study guide for students to place in their folders. After studying the cover and/or glancing through the book or chapter titles, students can participate in several pre-reading activities. Vocabulary questions should be considered before reading of a chapter; all other work should be done after the chapter has been read. Comprehension questions can be answered orally or in writing. The classroom teacher should decide on the amount of work to be assigned, nurture the readers, and inspire students' love of reading.

Using a novel to a lesson plan is numerous. Students read good literature in the original form, rather than in a summary or edited form. Good reading habits can be formed by repetitive practice and focusing on interpretive comprehension and literary techniques. This will transfer to any book students choose to read. The goal is for passive readers to become active and avid readers.

Special Thanks to Jeff Simpson, MEd, and taught for over thirty years, for his input and editing of this Study Guide. ME Drewry has a degree in General Education and Special Education, and has been teaching for a number of years, and is a reading specialist.

Imprint
The Headless Oxman Study Guide
PK Burian & ME Drewry
Copyright: © 2014 Patricia Azeltine & Mary Drewry
ISBN 978-1500910686

PRE-READING ACTIVITIES

1. Preview the book by reading the title and by looking at the illustration on the cover. What do you think this book will be about? Do you think it will be serious or humorous? Do you think it will be a mystery, adventure, romance, fantasy, historical, or fairy tale? Can the book be a combination of these types of books?

2. Would you ever consider going into a graveyard at night? In the chart below write an "X" in the column showing your response in each situation.

	Definitely	Maybe	No Way!
To dig up a dead body.			
To hunt for ghosts.			
Go into the graveyard on a dare.			
Go to a burial or funeral.			
Put in your idea for going into a graveyard at night.			

* * *

3. The word "grave" can be used in several different ways. Think of what a grave is. Think of what a grave is normally used for. Now try to explain the meaning of the expressions below.

1. As the boat was sinking Thomas found himself <u>in a grave situation</u>.

_____

_____

2. Aunt Matilda's casket was lowered <u>into a deep, dirt grave</u>.

_____

_____

Pre-Reading Activities continued…

3. Eddie's so old he has <u>one foot in the grave</u>.

    _____

    _____

4. If you color your hair purple, your grandmother will <u>turn over in her grave</u>.

    _____

<u>Interesting fact</u>: In a burial site found in 1957-1961 in the valley of the Great Zab in the Kurdistan Region of Iraq, an archaeologist discovered Neanderthal graves. It is believed Neanderthals buried their dead. The skeletons dated from 60,000 – 80,000 years BP (Before Present) times.

Name: _____

Chapter 1:

Vocabulary: Draw a line from each word on the left to its definition on the right.

<u>**Column I**</u>   <u>**Column II**</u>

1. rippled   a. lingered about or wait near at hand.

2. mimicked   b. said in a dull, continued, monotonous sound.

3. droned   c. rose and fell in repeatedly.

4. engraved   d. stretched out one's neck.

5. hovered   e. copied in action or speech.

6. craned   f. impressed deeply on a hard surface of metal, stone,

* * *

Use the numbered words in Column I to fill in the blanks below. Choose the word that would best fit in the blanks in the sentences below.

1. The helicopter _____ above the landing pad before it came to a safe stop.

2. The salesman _____ on and on about his product, until I thought I'd fall asleep.

3. My little sister _____ everything I said and did like a shadow.

4. The music the orchestra played _____ to the back of the auditorium.

5. I stretched and _____ my neck to see around the adults in front of me at the parade.

6. My first place trophy had my name _____ on it.

Chapter 1 continued ….

Chapter Questions:

1. What happens at the unveiling that shocks the crowd?

   _____

   _____

2. What does Daytona and Laura bet Jesse, Austin and Poe?

   _____

   _____

3. Is the town of Mason an old town or a newer town?

   _____

   _____

4. Did Jess find evidence of the man in the alleyway?

   _____

   _____

Discussion Questions:

1. What skills would you need to be a good detective?

2. Why would a police detective need the following skills? A. Ability to talk with people, and calm them down if they are upset. B. Communicate clearly, so people understand them. C. Make people understand what the detective is trying to accomplish.

3. Why would writing skills be important for a detective?

Chapter 1 continued...

Writing Activity:

1. Jesse sees a tall man with his legs crossed at the ankles and wearing jeans standing in the alley, but the shadows hide the rest of him. Describe what you think this man might look like i.e. face, body, clothes).

    _____

    _____

    _____

    _____

2. Jesse peers into the J.R. Dixon Building. It's an empty building. What do you think the building was used for? Was it an old factory? If so, what do you think the factory made? Or was it a clothing store or used for something else?

    _____

    _____

Interesting facts: The oldest "buildings" in the United States are found in New Mexico with the Native American Pueblo Indians. These structures date back to 750 CE. These Native Americans built towns, played organized sports, excelled at hunting and fishing, and had a democratic government structure. They were experts at farming, and women held important roles in their society. These buildings have been considered part of the United States since 1848, when New Mexico was annexed into the Union. These buildings can be found all over America's Southwest in New Mexico, Texas, Colorado, Utah, Nevada, and Arizona.

Chapters 2 & 3

Vocabulary: Synonyms are words that have similar meanings. Use a dictionary and draw a line from each word in Column I to its synonym in Column II.

Column I	Column II
1. assaulted	a. remembered
2. echoed	b. poured
3. retained	c. changed
4. morphed	d. attacked
5. funneled	e. fell
6. collapsed	f. sounded

Use the words in Column I to fill in the blanks in the sentences below.

1. Mom _____ the sugar into a bowl.

2. My voice _____ off the walls of the canyon.

3. When John punched Tom he _____ him.

4. The caterpillar _____ into a beautiful butterfly.

5. The explosion _____ the bridge.

6. Sarah _____ secret information from a week ago.

Discussion Questions:

1.   What clues lead Jesse to the door of the J. R. Dixon Building? Which of his senses did he use to figure out these clues?

   _____

Chapters 2 & 3 continued…

_____

2. What does Austin do when the owner of the J. R. Dixon Building catches them in there? What could he have done differently?

_____

_____

3.

What do the boys learn from the old letter they find in the peacock's room upstairs in the J. R. Dixon Building? How will this help in finding the head?

_____

_____

Multiple Choice: Choose the BEST answer for each of the following sentences.

1. What does Jesse, Austin, and Poe find in the old wood stove in the J. R. Dixon Building?
    a. the statue of Jebediah Mason's head.
    b. a chard piece of wood.
    c. nothing, the stove was empty.
2. When Jesse searched the main room on the first floor of the J. R. Dixon Building, where did he look for the statue's head?
    a. behind the counter.
    b. in a ceramic flower pot.
    c. in the storage closet.
    d. all of the above.
3. What does Jesse borrow from Austin to open the air vent?
    a. a screw driver.
    b. Whoopie Cool pocket knife.
    c. Whatchamacallit Do-dad.
    d. a fingernail file.
4. What does Austin find in the upstairs bedroom?
    a. peacocks.
    b. an empty room.
    c. a bed and furniture.

Chapters 2 & 3 continued...

5. Who did the boys hide from in the peacock room?
    a. the police.
    b. the building owner.
    c. Daytona and Laura.
6. What did Poe accidentally leave in his pocket after they ran out of the J. R. Dixon Building?
    a. the Whatchamacallit Do-dad.
    b. a letter from Jonathan Dixon to his wife.
    c. his cell phone.
    d. his homework.

Writing Activity: Write about a time when you got in trouble for doing something you shouldn't have been doing. Were you in a place you didn't belong? Describe how you felt. How did your body react when you got caught? Did you sweat, shake, shiver, or laugh? Explain.

Interesting Facts: Preserving old photographs and letters is best done in a climate-controlled environment. It is best if it is air-conditioned, a dark room, or a safe, like a safe deposit box in a bank. The best temperature is 68°F (20°C). Place your photographs or letters in an acid-free album or box. You can also use Mylar film, an acid-free polyester film. Dust the letters and photographs with a clean, dry cloth. Avoid using water. If you store them in a folder, use a plastic folder from polyester, polypropylene, or polyethylene. Do not use PVC (polyvinyl chloride) plastic because it will break down your photographs and letters and cause irreparable damage. Why acid-free? Paper is made from wood pulp which has lignin in it. This causes paper to turn yellow, become brittle, and deteriorate over time. Light and heat will cause the paper to break down faster.

Chapters 4 & 5

Vocabulary: Antonyms are words of opposite meanings. For example, the word "sad" would be the antonym to the word "happy." Draw a line from each word in Column I to its antonym (opposite meaning) in Column II.

<u>Column I</u>

1. public
2. finished
3. appeared
4. wrinkled
5. decay
6. moisture

<u>Column II</u>

a. started
b. smoothed
c. refreshed
d. private
e. vanished
f. dry

Use these words in Column I to fill in the blanks in the sentences found in the book.

1. Jesse, Austin, and Poe dumped their garbage bags at the nearest _____ trash can.
2. In fact, it'll suck the _____ out of the body and help to preserve it.
3. He could speed-read, and probably _____ the page in seconds flat.
4. It is true that gardeners' limestone will help _____ compost, but it does nothing to decompose a human body.
5. I waited for the results. One article _____. We crowded around the monitor to read it.
6. Poe _____ his nose

Discussion Questions:

1. What are Jesse, Austin, and Poe searching for in the newspaper office? How will that help them find the treasure?

   _____

   _____

2. Where do the boys go to look for the dead body of Jonathan Dixon? Do they find him? What clues led them to look there?

   _____

   _____

Chapters 4 & 5 continued…

3. What happens to Austin after the peacock chases him down the hallway? How would you react to being chased by peacocks?

_____

_____

Science Connection: Look up on the computer how to make a flashlight and find different ways to make it. Fill in the chart to list the items you need to make the one you found. Then fill in the blanks to list the items you would need to make your own flashlight.

Items for Jesse's flashlight	Items needed for the flashlight on the computer	Your flashlight
Duct Tape		
Foil		
Batteries		
Light bulb		
Dental floss		
Match sticks (wooden ones)		

Writing Activities: Do you think your flashlight would light up? Why or why not?

Interesting facts: peacocks are known as peafowl. They are best known for their spread of tail feathers. The male is called a peacock and the female is a penhen. Their offspring are called peachicks. They are part of the pheasant family.

Chapters 6 & 7

Vocabulary: For each word listed, write down your definition of the word. Then read the sentence it comes from in the book and decided which definition listed below is the correct one. Circle your answer.

1. Triumphantly. Your
   definition:_____

   "Daytona and Laura strutted in, reminding me of the two peacocks upstairs. They were smirking <u>triumphantly</u>."
   a. the ability to play a musical instrument.
   b. having achieved victory or success.
   c. a compliment given to someone.

2. Babbling. Your definition:
   _____

   "I opened my mouth to answer, but Austin cut me off, <u>babbling</u>, once again, like an auctioneer."
   a. foolish or meaningless chatter; prattle.
   b. tripping or falling over something.
   c. to make your point very clear.

3. Traumatic. Your definition:
   _____

   "I think my dad had called it something like Post <u>Traumatic</u> Stress. I'm not sure what that is, but it must be pretty bad to make a person homeless."

   a. a happy event; or something that creates happiness.
   b. the act of being changed into form, substance, or condition.
   c. of, pertaining to, or produced by a trauma or wound; psychologically painful.

4. Speculation. Your definition:
   _____

   "My dad would call our guesses <u>speculation</u>, because we couldn't prove anything we're saying. We don't have any facts yet."
   a. to engage in conjectural thought or reflection; a conclusion or opinion.
   b. dramatically daring or thrilling.
   c. a brilliant idea.

Chapters 6 & 7 continued...

5. Discouraged. Your definition:

    _____

    "A map that no one can read. It's faded too much over time." Poe sounded
    <u>discouraged</u>."
    a. lack of harmony.
    b. to think unworthy of notice or performance.
    c. to deprive of courage, hope, or confidence; dishearten.

6. Precious. Your definition:

    _____

    "She was a really good cook," Maggie said. "In fact, she called her cast iron pot her
     most <u>precious</u> possession."
    a. old and worn out.
    b. high priced or great value; very valuable.
    c. something that sets an example for or will be used in the future.

Chapter Questions:

1. How does Jesse know the skeleton is Jonathan Dixon? What detective skills is he
    using?

    _____

    _____

2. Where and how do Jesse, Austin, and Poe find the first clue to the treasure? What did
    they do wrong in finding this clue?

    _____

    _____

Interesting facts: Bricks are one of the oldest known building
materials and date back to 7000 BC. Bricks were sun dried mud.
Fired bricks were found to be more resistant to weather conditions,
which is why they were used for permanent buildings and still are.
Fired bricks are also known for absorbing heat throughout the day
and releasing it at night.

Chapters 6 & 7 continued...

Literary Activity: A definition is the meaning of a word. A synonym is a word having the same or similar meaning. An antonym is a word's opposite meaning. Select three words from the box and write what your definition for the word is; three synonyms; then three antonyms; and then look the word up in the dictionary and thesaurus and see if your answers are correct.

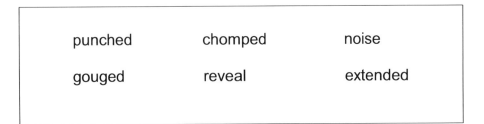

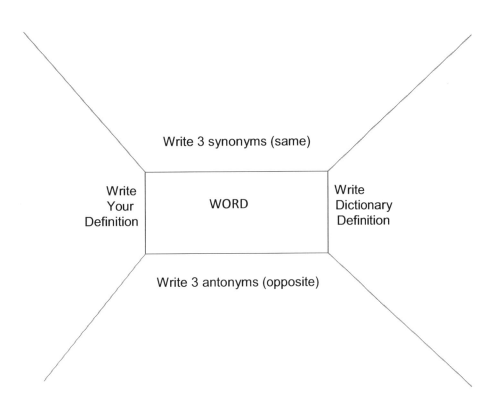

Writing Acitivity: Why did Jesse lie to his friends about losing his lunch? Try and use some of the words in the box at the top of the page, synonyms, or antonyms that you found for your three words in your answer.

Chapters 8 & 9

Vocabulary: Draw a line from each word on the left to its definition on the right.

1. suspicious
2. motioned
3. alibi
4. tedious

5. emphasize
6. potential

a. the act or process of moving; movement.
b. boring or too slow or long; dull.
c. to give special attention to something; feature.
d. causing a feeling that something is wrong or that someone is behaving wrongly; distrustful.
e. capable of becoming real; possible.
f. a claim that you cannot be guilty of a crime because you were somewhere else when the crime was committed; defense.

* * *

Fill-in Sentences: Use the numbered words to fill in the blanks.

1. I stepped on to the top of the pile of bricks to begin the _____ work of checking each one, when I heard a low menacing growl behind me.

2. He shook his head as if to _____ his answer.

3. "If it wasn't for a _____ lawsuit, I'd make you pay for it."

4. "The good news is that the building is still standing," Poe said. "The bad news is that it's going to be hard to find the brick without looking _____."

5. I spotted Poe and _____ for him to come to me.

6. "Oh, by the way, we got three sets of prints off the statue head. Two kids prints and one adult. The adult turned out to be a construction worker the City hired to put up the statue. He had an _____ for the night before the unveiling."

Discussion Questions:

1. When Jesse rearranges the letters found on the two clues (i.e., URCH, CHUR, RUCH, and RHUC) he can't figure out what they mean. What do you think they represent?

_____

_____

Chapter 8 & 9 continued…

2. At the pile of bricks what does Jesse find and where does it take them next?

    _____

    _____

Language Study: Anagrams

Anagrams are words formed by rearranging the letters of another word. Example, by rearranging the word "thing" you can create the word "night" made up of the same letters. So let's try creating anagrams from the words found in book and listed below.

1. from: _____. (Hint: the shape of something).

2. spot: _____.(Hint: high in quality, ability, popularity).

3. stops: _____.(Hint: pillars or columns).

4. waits: _____.(Hint: middle part of your body).

5. what: _____.(Hint: to stop being frozen).

6. moor: _____.(Hint: where someone sleeps in a house).

7. race: _____.(Hint: to keep something in good
                                            condition).

8. night: _____.(Hint: an object, animal, quality, of any kind).

9. bat: _____.(Hint: a small flap or loop to pull).

10 low: _____.(Hint: a large wild animal that is dog like).

Chapter 8 & 9 continued...

Word Study: The words listed below are types of jobs that require specialized education, training, or skill. Match the job to the definition by writing the word in the blank.

cop	coroner	curator
detective	mayor	proprietor

_____ 1. A person who is in charge of a museum.

_____ 2. A person who finds hidden or unknown information related to crimes.

_____ 3. A person who enforces the law at a local level.

_____ 4. A person who owns a business or property.

_____ 5. A person elected to head the government of a city or town.

_____ 6. A public official who finds out the cause of death when people die suddenly.

Science Connection: We use our senses every day and don't even realize it. When Jesse goes to the cemetery at night he uses his sense.

Sight: Jesse sees the moon shining brightly in the clear sky.

Sound: Jesse hears the leaves scraping over the concete.

Smell: Jesse smells smoke coming from someone's chimney.

Taste: After holding his breath, Jesse exhales.

Touch: Jesse feels the smooth texture of the glass jug that holds the gold.

Select one of the senses. Find a diagram or draw what body part uses that sense. Explain how does this sense work?

Interesting fact: Did you know that when a person dies, hearing is the last sense you lose. The first sense you lose is sight.

Name: _____

Writing Activity: Describe how you use your senses every day in your classroom. What do you see? What do you hear? Do you smell anything? Do you taste anything? What do you touch and what is the texture of what you are touching?

Interesting facts: The first museum dated back to circa 530 BCE, called Ennigaldi-Nanna's Museum. The curator of the museum was Princess Ennigaldi, the daughter of Nabonidus, the last king of the Neo-Babylonian Empire, located in Ur, which is in modern-day Iraq. Many artifacts were found already labeled.

Name: _____

Chapter 10 & 11

Vocabulary: For each word determine if it is a noun, verb, adjective, or adverb. Write the word in the appropriate column. Could some of these words be listed in more than one column?

impatiently	obliged	irritate	sinister
casket	appreciate	silhouette	illegal
arched	ancestor	donation	generous

Noun	Verb	Adjective	Adverb

Write a sentence for the following words:

1. Permission (noun): _____.

2. Responsible (adjective): _____.

3. Serious (adjective): _____.

4. Honesty (noun): _____.

Discussion Questions:

1. The boys dream of what they would buy with the gold. Austin wanted to build a candy factory. Jesse wanted to build a baseball park. And Poe wanted to give his parents money so his dad could stay home. What would you do with a pot of gold? How would it affect those around you?

2. In the cemetery the boys think they see a ghost, but it turns out to be Bill, the homeless man. Describe what you think a ghost would look like.

Name: _____

Chapters 10 & 11 continued….

Literary Activity: Compare the boys to the girls in the Venn Diagram. In the <u>intersecting</u> of the circles list what is <u>similar</u> between the boys and girls. On the outside of the circles, list the boys and girls characteristics that are different. Ex. Boys: irresponsible (cleanup duties), Girls: responsible (cleanup duties), and both are curious.

Boys: Jesse, Austin & Poe   Girls: Daytona & Laura

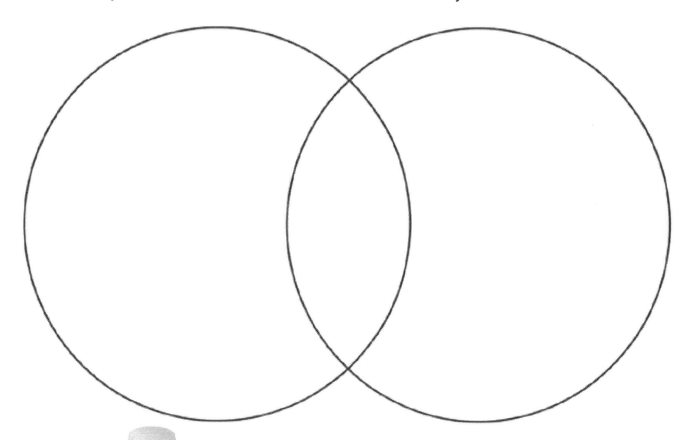

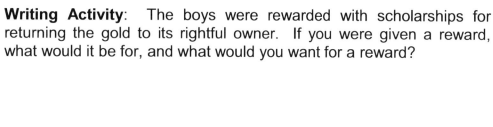

Writing Activity: The boys were rewarded with scholarships for returning the gold to its rightful owner. If you were given a reward, what would it be for, and what would you want for a reward?

Interesting facts: Gold is a chemical element with the symbol <u>**Au**</u>, and an atomic number of 79. Gold is dense, soft, and can be shaped. It is bright in color and luster. It will not tarnish in air or water. It is used for coins, jewelry, and other arts. Gold is the only metal that does not rust, even if it is buried in the ground for thousands of years.

Fun Activities:

Word Search

Line through or circle the hidden words in the puzzle. The first word is done for you.

Words
Alibi
Arched
Austin
Casket
Chomped
Craned
Cop
Curator
Decay
Echo
Holmes
Illegal
Irritate
Jesse
Noise
Poe
Reveal
Vent

```
A  L  I  B  I  X  P  R  Z  I
L  R  S  C  R  A  N  E  D  L
N  O  E  Z  R  U  O  V  E  L
U  T  M  R  I  S  I  E  P  E
A  A  L  F  T  T  S  A  M  G
R  R  O  O  A  I  E  L  O  A
C  U  H  K  T  N  E  V  H  L
H  C  G  T  E  K  S  A  C  P
E  S  S  E  J  Q  Y  H  O  O
D  E  C  A  Y  V  X  C  M  E
```

Fun Activities:

Block Word Search

Each word is hidden in the puzzle in a box or rectangle. The letters of the word might be listed clock-wise or counter-clock-wise. One word has been boxed for you.

<u>Words</u>

Appear
Babbling
Collapse
Donation
Droned
Extend
Funnel
Gold
Precious
Retain
Sinister
Trauma

```
S  I  E  X  U  L  Z  D  R  O
R  N  D  T  S  T  Q  D  E  N
E  I  N  E  S  E  P  T  M  S
T  S  X  B  A  D  G  F  U  N
M  A  T  G  B  L  O  L  E  N
U  A  R  N  B  A  D  O  B  C
P  R  E  I  L  D  N  N  L  A
S  E  T  A  P  P  O  A  L  P
U  C  F  R  A  E  I  T  O  S
O  I  G  J  I  L  K  H  C  E
```

Name: _____

Fun Activities:

Synonym Crossword Puzzle

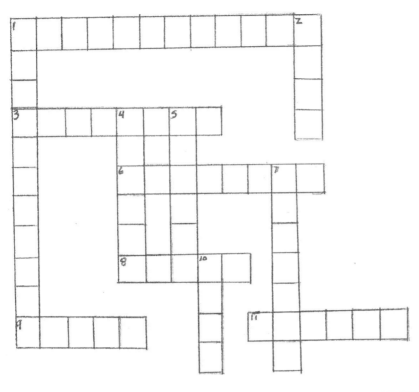

Search	Needed	Treasure	Gold
Speculation	Nudge	Park	Newer
Ceremony	Motion	Rambled	Scholarship

The words in the box fit into the crossword puzzle. Their synonym is listed below. Determine which synonym fits the words in the box, and then write that word in the crossword puzzle.

Down
1 Consideration, thought
2 Outdoor place
4 Movement
5 Necessary, wanted
7 Spoke
10 Yellow ore

Across
1 Award
3 Celebration
5 Prize, riches
8 Poke, bump, push
9 Fresh, current
11 Hunt, seek

Fun Activities:

Antonym Word Scramble

Perfect	Vain	Common	Public	Noise
Resist	Myth	Mumble	Drift	Fragile

In the words listed below, unscramble the antonym of the word listed in the box.

COMPLY. Antonym: RTIESS Answer: ___ ___ ___ ___ ___ ___

SHOUT. Antonym: BMUMLE Answer: ___ ___ ___ ___ ___ ___

STEER. Antonym: DRTFI Answer: ___ ___ ___ ___ ___

PRIVATE. Antonym: PUBCLI Answer: ___ ___ ___ ___ ___ ___

UNIQUE. Antonym: MOCMON Answer: ___ ___ ___ ___ ___ ___

HUMBLE. Antonym: NVIA Answer: ___ ___ ___ ___

FACT. Antonym: THYM Answer: ___ ___ ___ ___

SILENCE. Antonym: SOINE Answer: ___ ___ ___ ___ ___

RUINED. Antonym: FERPETC Answer: ___ ___ ___ ___ ___ ___ ___

STURDY. Antonym: GRAFILE Answer: ___ ___ ___ ___ ___ ___ ___

Answer Key

Chapter 1

Vocabulary: 1. c 2. e 3. b 4. f 5. a 6. d; 1. hovered 2. droned 3. mimicked 4. rippled 5. craned 6. engraved.

Chapter Questions: 1. At the unveiling the crowd is shocked because the statues' head of Zachariah Mason is chopped off. 2. Daytona and Laura bet Jesse, Austin, and Poe that they can find the statue's head first. 3. The town of Mason is an older town, founded after the gold rush in Alaska in 1896. 4. Jesse does not find evidence of the man he sees in the alleyway.

Discussion Questions: 1. Skills needed to be a good police detective are good eye for detail, good memory, good reasoning, paying attention to what is happening, know how to find information, ask good questions, blend in the crowd, keep good notes, good communications with public and peers. 2. A. Often when people are upset they may make a situation worse. By calming them down, a detective may find out what the problem is and resolve or investigate it further. B. Communication, whether it is in writing or verbally is one of the most important skills a detective can develop. He needs to convey clearly to everyone involved what is going on and what needs to be done. C. Sometimes, if witnesses know what the detective needs from them, then they will relax and open up more. 3. Writing skills are very important to a detective because they have to write down in a report what they have seen and what has taken place. If their writing is poor, it could mean a criminal getting off.

Chapter 2 & 3

Vocabulary: 1. d 2. f 3. a 4. c 5. b 6. e; 1. funneled 2. echoing 3. assaulted 4. morphed 5. collapsed 6. retained.

Discussion Questions: 1. The clues that lead Jesse to the door of the J.R. Dixon Building were the splatters of red paint, smell of paint, scratched marks on front door that looked fresh and recent, and the paint was the same color as the paint dripping on the neck of the statue of Zachariah Mason. The senses he used was sight, smell, and touch. 2. When the owner of the J.R. Dixon Building catches the gang in his building Austin confesses to everything they did, talking very fast. 3. In the letter the boys find in the peacock room, they learn that Zachariah Mason possibly murdered Jonathan Dixon, and that Jonathan hid his gold so Zachariah could never find it.

Multiple Choice: 1. b 2. d 3. c 4. a 5. c 6. b

Chapters 4 & 5

Vocabulary: 1. d 2. a 3. e 4. b 5. c 6. f; 1. public 2. moisture 3. finished 4. decay 5. appeared 6. wrinkled.

Discussion Questions: 1. Jesse, Austin, and Poe are searching in the newspaper office for clues of where the gold might be hidden. 2. The boys go look for the dead body of Jonathan Dixon in the J.R. Dixon Building because it used to be a mortuary (funeral home). Their search first comes up empty, but then they accidentally find him under the stairs. 3. After the peacocks chase Austin down the hallway he falls through the loose step on the stairs and gets stuck.

Chapter 6 & 7

Vocabulary: 1. b 2. a 3. c 4. a 5. b 6. b;

Chapter Questions: 1. Jesse knows the skeleton is Jonathan Dixon because he remembered seeing Jonathan wearing the same clothes in a photograph they looked at. The detective skills Jesse is using are observation, memory, and analytical. 2. Jesse, Austin, and Poe found the first clue to the treasure in the Mason Historical Museum's exhibit of Betsy Dixon's stirring spoon. The spoon was hollowed out and the clue was inside the handle. The boys were wrong to climb into the exhibit and handle the antique items.

Chapter 8 & 9

Vocabulary: 1. d 2. a 3. f 4. b 5. c 6. e; 1. tedious 2. emphasize 3. potential 4. suspicious 5. motioned 6. alibi

Discussion Questions: 1. The four letters C-H-U-R could stand for anything. We find out when they get the last clue it spells out CHURCH. CHURCH could represent a person, place, or thing—a name of a street, a building, a person's name, a secret code, or many other possibilities. 2. At the pile of bricks Jesse finds a brick in a triangle shape, or shape of a piece of pie. On the brick, it gives them two more letters CH, which completes the word CHURCH. This takes them to the cemetery where a small church stands.

Language Study: 1. form 2. tops 3. post 4. waist 5. thaw 6. room 7. care 8. thing 9. tab 10. wolf.

Word Study: 1. curator 2. detective 3. cop 4. proprietor 5. mayor 6. coroner

Chapter 10 & 11

Vocabulary: impatiently (adjective), irritate (verb), sinister (adjective), casket (noun and verb), silhouette (noun and verb), illegal (adjective and noun), arched (adjective), ancestor (noun), donation (noun), generous (adjective), easily (adverb), noisily (adverb); 1. Tommy was refused permission (noun) to go to the bathroom. 2. Cathy was responsible (adjective) for the dogs getting out of the yard. 3. Howard was a serious (adjective) card player. 4. In all honesty (noun), I would never go to that restaurant again.

Name: _____

Fun Pages

Word Search Answer Page

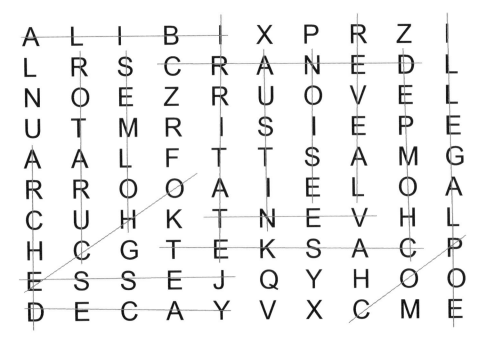

Block Word Search Answer Page

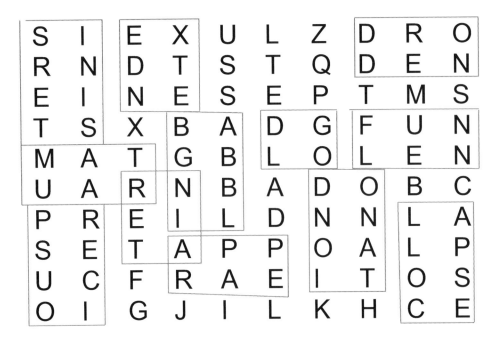

Fun Activities

Synonym Crossword Puzzle Answer Page

<u>Down</u>
1 speculation
2 park
4 motion
5 needed
7 rambled
10 gold

<u>Across</u>
1 scholarship
3 ceremony
6 treasure
8 nudge
9 newer
11 search

Antonym Word Scramble Answer Page

COMPLY. Antonym: RTIESS Answer: RESIST.

SHOUT. Antonym: BMUMLE   Answer: MUMBLE.

STEER. Antonym: DRTFI Answer: DRIFT.

PRIVATE. Antonym: PUBCLI Answer: PUBLIC.

UNIQUE. Antonym: MOCERAP Answer: COMMON.

HUMBLE. Antonym: NVIA Answer: VAIN.

FACT. Antonym: THYM Answer: MYTH.

SILENCE. Antonym: SOINE Answer: NOISE.

RUINED. Antonym: FERPETC Answer: PERFECT.

STURDY. Antonym: GRAFILE Answer: FRAGILE.

41661245R00019

Made in the USA
Charleston, SC
08 May 2015